At sea

Gannet
This beautiful bird is usually seen off shore rearing up into the sky and then diving headlong into a shoal of fish - hitting the water at as much as 30 m.p.h. Breeds on islands off the Welsh coast.

Puffin
This adorably comic bird breeds in burrows on Annet & some of the smaller islands such as Men-a-vaur & Scilly Rock. Special boat trips are often arranged to watch these birds. Can be seen from Spring to the end of July.

Manx Shearwater
Superbly adapted for a life at sea skimming the tops of waves but completely unable to land gracefully on shore. Its landing technique simply seems to involve colliding with the ground. Special boat trips to watch them as they come to land in the evening on Annet. There is a great cacophony as they establish the whereabouts of their mates and burrows.

European Storm Petrel
Breeds on Annet but are rarely seen during the day, except when it comes inshore to shelter from an oncoming storm - hence its name and reputation as a sign of bad weather to come.

Rocky habitats

Guillemot
Increasingly rare auk. Breeds on exposed rocky ledges on Men-a-vaur.

Cormorant & Shag
Closely related species. The cormorant has a white face patch. The shag is one of the most commonly spotted birds on the Scillies - especially in the shallow water between the islands where it sits on the surface, periodically diving to chase fish underwater. Usually spotted standing on rocks and buoys in this characteristic pose - drying out its wings between fishing trips.

Razorbill
Breeds in crevices between rocks on the more inhospitable islands. A member of the auk family.

Kittiwake
Spends most of the year out at sea. Breeds on sheltered cliff faces on Tresco & some of the other smaller islands.

Great Black Backed Gull
Definitely a bird with 'attitude'. The charcoal back and wings give it a regal presence. It rarely seems to bother with human scraps instead preferring to feed on other birds and their chicks.

Herring Gull
The most common gull on our coasts and a prolific scavenger. It has adapted well to take advantage of the rubbish thrown away by man.

VISITOR INFORMATION

The Isles of Scilly lie about 30 miles southwest of Land's End in Cornwall. There are five inhabited islands all with accommodation. St Mary's is the main island. Although there are roads on the islands it is not possible to bring your own car to Scilly.

Isles of Scilly Tourist Information Centre

Hugh Street, Hugh Town, St Mary's. Tel: (01720) 422536

HOW TO GET TO THE ISLANDS

Frequent daily trains run directly to Penzance from London Paddington and the North. A sleeper service operates from London Paddington.

Helicopter

Flights leave from the Heliport just outside Penzance. Secure parking on site. There is a connecting bus service from the train station to the heliport. Direct flights are available to St Mary's Airport and Tresco - the flight lasts about 20 mins.

Ship

The Scillonian III leaves from the Lighthouse Pier at Penzance Harbour. Long stay parking is available on the Harbour public car park opposite Penzance train station. Private secure parking is also available near the harbour. The trip takes about 2 hours.

Plane

The Isles of Scilly Skybus operates services from Bristol, Exeter, Southampton, Portsmouth, Newquay and St Just (9 miles from Penzance) to Mary's Airport. A connecting bus service runs from Penzance train station to St Just Airport. The flight lasts about 15 minutes.

Shipman Head

Bryher *p30*

Scilly Rock   Norrard

Norrard Gweal   Hotel
Rocks

Maiden Bower
Illiswilgig

Mincarlo   **Samson** *p27*

White Island

NORTH CHANNEL   Gt Mina

BROAD SOUND

Old Wreck Buoy

Gunners

Crim Rocks

Annet   Lower Town

Hellweathers

Gt Crebawethan *p23*

St Agnes *p18*

Bishop Rock Lighthouse

Western Rocks

Melledgan

Rosevear

Rosevean   Gorregan

Gilstone

ACTIVITIES

Sailing & Diving Tuition

Sailing tuition is available on most of the islands and there are diving centres on St Mary's and St Martin's. Contact the TIC for more information (see above).

GETTING AROUND THE ISLANDS

There is a frequent boat service between all the inhabited islands. The boats leave just after 10am in the morning and again at about 2pm in the afternoon. Return boats leave at lunchtime and late afternoon. Exact times and landing places are dependent on the tides (see individual island maps for details). On landing the boatman will let you know where he will pick you up. Other special excursions are common - to see the seals at the Western Rocks and Eastern Isles or to go puffin spotting at sea. There are popular evening trips to the Turk's Head on St Agnes. Notice boards on each island display the departure times and destinations of that day's and the next day's sailings. You can also book special trips to uninhabited islands for the day. Annet and some other islands with large populations of birds are closed to visitors during the breeding season.

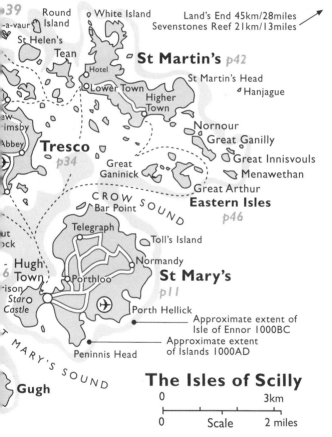

Pilot Gig Racing

Pilot gigs are six oared boats developed in the C19th to race competing pilots out to British bound sail ships. The first pilot to reach the ship would get the job to navigate it into port. This led to an intense rivalry between boats. The pilots are no longer required but the rivalry continues. Races happen every Wednesday and Friday evening in the Summer. Each island has its own boat & you can follow the race from a launch. The world championships are often held on Scilly, usually in May. The most common courses are from Nut Rock (Samson) to St Mary's and from Old Wreck Buoy (Annet) to St Mary's.

Introduction

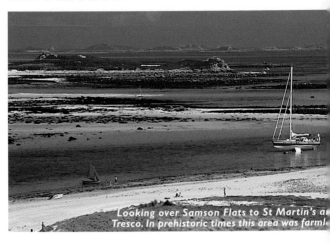

Looking over Samson Flats to St Martin's a
Tresco. In prehistoric times this area was farml

There is something about islands that appeals to the human spirit. It is the feeling of a world drawn at a smaller scale - everything on the islands seems a step down in size from the mainland. Even the birds, so wary on the mainland, are tame enough to eat out of your hand on Scilly. This gives you a wonderfully refreshing feeling of walking in an enchanted landscape. Children instinctively respond to this and love the Isles of Scilly. If there is a currency in happy childhood memories then the islands are certainly rich.

Life on Scilly, as on all islands, is governed by the sea and the tides. It dictates the practicalities of both leisure and business. This is especially true of the smaller off-islands which are inaccessible by boat on a low Spring tide, although surprisingly on this sort of tide you can actually walk between some of the islands across the exposed sand banks. As a result, life on the islands is as much centered on the lunar clock that controls the tides, as the 24 hour clock. The sea around the islands is in a constant state of change and motion. The tide can drop by as much as five metres in just six hours. That roughly equates to two billion tons of water on the move just in and around Scilly and accounts for the fierce currents that can race between the islands.

The heightened sense of the natural world is also evident in the way weather rolls in over the sea. Showers sweep across the sky and the horizon is always changing - sometimes sharply defined between sea and sky and sometimes melded into one. This awaking of the senses is nowhere more obvious than in the fabulous night skies. There is hardly any pollution to reduce the clarity of the stars on Scilly. The dusty band of the Milky Way is crystal clear and rolling home from the pub it sometimes feels as if you are being bombarded by shooting stars.

The five inhabited islands of Scilly all have their own character and you will soon find the island that suits you best. The three off-islands of St Agnes, Bryher and St Martin's are the most remote. Here the only traffic on the small concrete roads is the occasional tractor. Bryher feels the most rugged and will appeal to the romantic.

St Agnes is the most self contained and is said to appeal to the independent minded. St Martin's with its lush crescent bays and long beaches has a serene feel to it. Tresco and St Mary's are more of a halfway house between the mainland and the off-islands with 'proper' traffic and more day trippers but to call them 'busy' or 'crowded' would be ridiculous. Tresco has the world famous Abbey Gardens and St Mary's is perfect for the first time visitor as all the other islands are within easy reach by inter-island launch.

Lyonnesse and the drowned landscape

The granite mass that forms the Isles of Scilly is part of a chain of dome like intrusions of granite that run from Dartmoor in the east, to the undersea outcrop of Haig Frais forty miles northwest of the islands. These massive underground intrusions all occurred in response to a collision between continental plates in the earth's crust between 200 and 300 million years ago. The collision resulted in the formation of the Laurasian Mountains. The Scillonian granite was implanted and cooled many kilometres beneath these mountains and as the peaks have been eroded away over the eons the granite has become exposed at the surface.

The granite forms a distinctive landscape characterised by the towering carns that mark almost every headland. The granite here weathers into extraordinary shapes many such as the *Loaded Camel Rock* at Porth Hellick and the rocks of Peninnis Head on St Mary's mimic the shapes of animals or faces. Inland the granite soils are free draining but poor in nutrients and have to be 'sweetened' by shell sand and rotted seaweed.

Sea level has varied tremendously over geological time - falling levels being associated with periods of glaciation where vast quantities of water become locked up in ice caps. At the height of the most recent glaciation, 18,000 years ago, sea level was as much as seventy five metres below the present day level and ice sheets extended from the north pole to cover half of Britain.

Generations of Scillonians have been told of a lost land that once lay between the Isles of Scilly and Land's

End - the land of Lyonnesse. A land it is said, of handsome maids and strong men; of rich pastures and fertile meadows and the beautiful city of Lions. A turreted castle stood on what is now the Sevenstones reef and from the highest turret you could count the steeples of 140 graceful churches. All this was suddenly engulfed by the sea.

The Loaded Camel Rock above Porth Hellick on St Mary's. Other strange shaped rocks on the islands include the Pulpit, Monk's Cowl and Tooth Rock at Peninnis Head on St Mary's. See also photo of the Nag's Head in the section on St Agnes.

Sometimes late at night in the corner of a West Cornwall pub you may even overhear an old fisherman recounting stories of how on a calm day, with a still sea, you can just hear a mournful toll as the sea currents gently move the bells in their steeples. Only one man and his horse survived the sudden inundation that engulfed Lyonnesse. He was out hunting in the hills near to the present day Land's End. Weary from his exertions he fell asleep under a May tree only to be woken by a deep rumble that quickly grew into a terrifying roar as a gigantic wave rolled across the land from the west. He mounted his horse and they galloped for their lives up the slope to high ground and safety but not before the horse lost a shoe in the scramble. There is a family in West Cornwall today whose coat of arms consists of three horseshoes and they claim to be directly descended from the single survivor of the flood that engulfed Lyonnesse.

Submerged field boundary from the first settlers on Scilly - probably Bronze Age. The boulders have been battered by sea and tide but are still clearly part of a linear man made structure. These walls criss-cross the sand flats between the four largest islands. Before submergence they were part of an inland agricultural landscape probably based around cereal cultivation and cattle rearing.

The legend may have grown taller with every telling but there are indeed traces of a lost society, their homes and fields now under the sea. We now know these are the homes of Bronze Age Scillonians who colonised Scilly 4,000 years ago when the four largest present day islands were connected by a now submerged central plain. Even today it is possible to wade between Tresco and Samson on a low Spring tide in August (see back cover). The tales of the fishermen must have been fuelled by seeing these submerged round houses and field walls. They now lie, tumbled and seaweed covered underwater between the islands and can also be seen on the foreshore of Green Bay on Bryher and at Pentle Bay on Tresco.

The first Scillonians

We know from archaeological evidence that the first humans to reach Scilly were the Mesolithic peoples (8000BC-4000BC). They moved north from the Mediterranean after the end of the last ice age 10,000 years ago probably following herds of migrating animals as the ice retreated. We have little evidence of how these people lived except that they probably lived a semi-transient life rather like native American Indians of the C19th. If they did roam here, then most of their camps

A reconstructed roundhouse adjacent to Bodrifty Ancient Village in West Cornwall. The remains of round houses are common both on the islands and on the sand flats between them.

are now lost to the sea as there is no trace of them on the present islands. At the start of the Mesolithic Age there was probably still enough water held in the ice caps for Scilly to still be connected to the mainland but by 4000BC Scilly had become a single island, with a wooded interior populated with deer and wild boar.

The Neolithic peoples (4000BC-2500BC) are the first people to really leave a mark on the landscape. They lived a more settled life than the Mesolithic hunters, cultivating cereals, domesticating animals as well as hunting and gathering. They shared a common culture with the other peoples of the Atlantic seaboard from Spain, Brittany through Cornwall to Wales and Ireland. In West Cornwall they built the large 'table like' quoits such as Lanyon and Mulfra Quoit near Penzance. The entrance graves so characteristic of Scilly probably have their origins in the beliefs of this period and there is some evidence to suggest that Scilly was cultivated in a very limited way at this time.

It's not until the Bronze Age (2,500BC-700BC) that the islands seem to come under sustained and widespread cultivation. The land was cleared of stones - some piled in circular mounds or cairns as on Shipman Head Down on Bryher. They cut down the wild wood and settled in villages of small round houses or hut circles. The stone foundations of these houses are common throughout the islands (although often hidden by bracken) and also show up as seaweed covered circles in the sandy, shallow sea between the islands. They are particularly obvious when seen from the helicopter as it comes in to land at Tresco.

It was these people who built the entrance graves that sit on almost every hilltop on the islands. Over seventy examples are documented on the islands. This is a type of tomb only found in Scilly and West Cornwall and they echo the more elaborate passage graves of Ireland and Brittany. They are often aligned together in 'family' groups on the crests of prominent hills such as North & South

Hill on Samson, Cruther's Hill on St Martin's, the north end of Gugh and on Porth Hellick Down on St Mary's. The best individual examples are at Innisidgen and Porth Hellick Down on St Mary's. There is evidence of both cremation, with the remains placed in pottery urns and simple internment with the bodies allowed to disintegrate naturally. This probably reflects that the entrance graves were often used over long periods. Entrance graves are often found linked by low field walls and it has been suggested that they may have had a function associated with fertility of the soil, perhaps in response to the exhaustion of the soil by poor farming practice.

Bronze Age entrance grave on the south hill of Samson. A speciality of the Isles of Scilly and West Cornwall. Fragments of burnt human bone were found at Knackyboy Carn entrance grave on St Martin's when it was excavated in the 1950's. Seventy pottery funeral urns were uncovered (some on view at the island museum). Alignments of entrance graves can be found on many hills on Scilly and notably on Cruther's Hill on St Martin's.

Towards the end of the Bronze Age cairns took over from entrance graves as the preferred funeral monuments. Cairns are essentially mounds of stones and they sometimes have a burial cist at their centre. Shipman Head Down on Bryher has an exceptionally large number of cairns. Other typical Bronze Age monuments are standing stones or menhirs. The best known on Scilly is the Old Man of Gugh, but there are several others including a statue menhir on Chapel Down, St Martin's.

During the Iron Age (700BC-400AD) there developed a sophisticated improvement on the common round house called the courtyard house (see page 14 for illustration). Once again, this type of building is unique to Scilly and West Cornwall. There is a good example at Halangy Down Ancient Village on St Mary's.

Cliff castles also date from this period - there are no spectacular examples on the islands but earth ramparts are visible at the Giant's Castle on St Mary's and at Boat Carn on Bryher. In the later period of the Iron Age Rome ruled Britain but this appears to have had a limited impact on the day to day lives of Celts in this remote part of Britain. The Romans seem to have upheld the Celtic status quo and Iron Age culture developed unhindered. In Scilly there seems to have been frequent contact probably with Roman trading ships. A Roman altar can be seen in the Abbey Gardens on Tresco and a Romano-British shrine was discovered on Nornour after storms exposed the remains of round houses at the head of the beach. The shrine was probably dedicated to a maritime goddess. That the Romans knew of Scilly there is little doubt. In 387AD two early Christian Bishops, Instantius and Tibericus were exiled here from Rome for the Prissillian heresy. They headed a cult of free love and of course being bishops, they insisted they got more free love, more often, than anyone else. When they arrived they probably found that if Christianity had taken root here at all it had already died out.

Chamber probably originally covered with stones and earth

Cremated remains placed in urns within passage. There is also some evidence of offerings of food and produce. Any precious grave goods have long been stolen.

Retaining kerb of upright stones

Bronze Age Entrance Grave

The departure of the Romans from Britain in C5th precipitated a slow decline in trade and commerce. The country split into a number of fractious small kingdoms. Christianity, which had spread with the Roman Empire had also declined. It was reestablished by missionaries from Wales and Ireland in the C7th and C8th, where it had always remained strong. The Celtic Christian tradition is a very different tradition to the Church of Rome. Its traditions are more like those of the Eastern Church, with emphasis on small monastic settlements and religious hermits. These men and women later became the Celtic saints and founded a number of small chapels on the islands (see sections on St Helen's and Tean).

The greatest threat to this way of life was the gradual rise in the sea level, with storms and storm surges inundating the low lying central plain of the Isle of Ennor. At sometime around the year 1000 the existing islands began to emerge from the sinking Ennor. The population of the islands at this point had probably fallen to a few hundred - many of those living a hand to mouth existence.

In 1120 Henry I granted all the churches on the northern part of Ennor to the Benedictine monks of Tavistock Abbey. The southern half of St Mary's and Agnes were granted to the Norman knight Richard de Wika. At this time Vikings and raiders from Ireland were a constant menace and eventually prompted the abandonment of Tresco Priory. Edward III granted the islands to the Black Prince, the first Duke of Cornwall, but Scilly was plagued by the twin threats of insecurity and the loss of the best agricultural land to the sea. For the next 400 years the islands seem to have sunk into obscurity.

A New Atlantic Age

The growth of sea trade on the new Atlantic trade routes to America and Africa from the Tudor period onwards once again brought the islands to the attention of national government. In order to safeguard the strategic position of Scilly fortifications were started, and in 1570 the islands were leased by the Duchy to the Godolphin family. At this time the islands were used as a base for privateers raiding the heavily laden ships heading home with valuable cargo. In Elizabethan times this piracy was ignored as long as it was to the detriment of Holland and France. The Spanish Armada had shown how vulnerable Scilly would be to any attack and so in 1593 Elizabeth I started to build the Star Castle on the Garrison.

During the English Civil War the islands were staunchly Royalist and Prince Charles stayed in the Star Castle in his flight from the Parliamentary forces in 1646. After subjugation by Parliament the islands rebelled in 1648 and took up attacking passing merchantman once more. In 1651 the toll on Dutch shipping prompted their government declare war on the islands - an act that was only withdrawn 20 years ago when the Dutch ambassador visited the islands to formally agree a peace. After the end of the Civil War Parliament encouraged a period of resettlement by families from the mainland.

By the end of the C18th and the beginning of the C19th life on Scilly was again at a low ebb. The Napoleonic Wars disrupted smuggling and fishing, both major sources of income for Scillonians. A series of poor harvests following the end of the Napoleonic wars brought a real prospect of famine. Pilotage fees for ships sailing to the major British ports gave some help but it was not enough to stop the islands falling into destitution. It fell to a visionary man called Augustus Smith to turn the situation around. He obtained the lease from the Duchy of Cornwall after the Godolphin family relinquished it in 1831 and set about reform. He insisted that the children should be well educated, a legacy continued to this day and he introduced new agricultural practices. The growth of the railways in the middle of the C19th brought tourists to the islands for the first time and also allowed the flower industry to flourish. For the first time cut flowers could now reach the London markets within a day and Scilly could exploit its early flowering season by suppling the London markets in the Winter.

Political instability in Europe at the beginning of the C20th caused the Government, ever mindful of the strategic position of the islands, to build new coastal batteries on the Garrison. During the First World War flying boats were stationed at Tresco and during the Second World War a squadron of Hurricanes were stationed on St Mary's to provide cover for convoys coming across the Atlantic.

Further reading:

The Archaeology of Scilly Cornwall Archaeological Unit
Exploration of a Drowned Landscape by Charles Thomas

Section 1.
St Mary's

St Mary's is the largest island in the Scillonian group. It's the ideal place to be based on your first trip to the islands as all the other smaller islands are easily accessible from here by inter-island boat service from the quay in Hugh Town - the main settlement with the majority of the shops, pubs and restaurants on the island. The island is a transitional stage between the mainland and the more remote off-islands such as Bryher and St Agnes. There are even places on St Mary's where you can't see the sea, which is most unusual on Scilly and probably explains why some off islanders regard St Mary's with the same sort of disdain they reserve for the mainland. Cars and buses are common on St Mary's whereas on the off-

Innisidgen Neolithic/Bronze Age Entrance Grave on the north of St Mary's. This type of tomb is only found in Scilly and West Cornwall.

islands tractors are the preferred form of transport. The sheltered centre of the island is mainly cultivated for flowers, particularly daffodils and other narcissi which are sent to London in early Spring. Vegetables and especially early potatoes are also widely cultivated.

It's possible to walk the coast of St Mary's in a single day but unless you are a seasoned walker, it's probably better to split the island up into smaller more manageable parts that can be covered in a single afternoon. The island bus service can drop you at the north end of the island so that you can then walk half the coast in either direction back to Hugh Town. In addition to the coast there are nature trails at Lower and Higher Moors. The Isles of Scilly Environmental Trust produce leaflets on the plant and birdlife on the trails. There are also popular evening strolls from Hugh Town to both Peninnis Head and the Garrison - see the next section.

St Mary's has many impressive prehistoric monuments. Scilly was on the main sea routes between the Bronze

► 14

Crow Rock

Bar Point

Wras

Pendrathen

Pendrathen
Quay

Halangy Point

Bant's Carn
Battery

Helvear

Bar Farm

Little Creeb
*Halangy
Porth*

Bristow

Halangy Down Ancient Village
Iron Age C7th BC - C1st AD

Longrock
Menhir

Higher
Trenoweth

Toll's Porth

Bant's Carn Entrance Grave
Bronze Age C25th BC-C7th BC

Pungies Lane

Higher
Newford

Lower
Newford

*Carn Morval
Down*

Telegraph

Content

Golf
Club

High L

Juliet's
Garden

Seaways Farm

Trewince

Porthloo

Porthloo

Heritage
Centre

Longsto

A3110

Boat
Yard

Mount Flagon/Harry's Wall's
Unfinished C16th Fortification

Four
Lanes
End

Carreg D
(garde

Sunnyside

*Thomas'
Porth*

Rocky Hill Lane

Rocky Hill
Farm

*Porth
Mellon*

Rose
Hill

A3111

Parting
Carn

Old Town Lane

Sandy Banks

Lower
Moors

Pottery

Isles of Scilly
Secondary School

Moor Well

A3112

High
Cross

Hugh Town

Church Road

Carn Gwarvel
Primary School

St Ma
Airpo

Hospital
& Health
Centre

A3112

Castle Farm

Nowhere

Old Town

Inner
Carn

King Edward

Old Town
Church

Slip
Old Quay

Porth
Minick

Buzza Hill Entrance Grave
Bronze Age C25th BC-C7th BC

Mainmark
Rock

*Stony
Porth*

Carn Leh

Gull Rock

Tolman H

Carn
Mahael

Peninnis Mill
(ruin)

Joe's Rock

Carn Leh
Cove

Inner To
Ledge

*Old Town
Bay*

Gilsto
Ledge

Pulpit Rock

Peninnis Head

Piper's
Hole

Carrickstarne

Inner Head

Gils

Potlard

Outer Head

Innisidgen

tle
rth

Innisidgen Entrance Graves
Bronze Age C25th BC-C7th BC

Innisidgen
Carn

sidgen
Hill

*Block House
Bay*

*The Scillonian III
berthed at Hugh
Town Quay*

Block House Point

*Watermill
Cove*

vear

Tregear's
Porth

Old
Quay

North
Pelistry

Pellow's Redoubt
Civil War Battery & Earthworks C17th

termill

Lane

Lenteverne

Toll's
Hill

Green
Farm

Toll's Island

termill

Kelp pits

South
Pelistry

orough
arm

Green Lane

Pelistry

Gilbert
Porth

Pelistry Bay

Maypole

Pelistry Lane

Pelistry Ledges

Holy Vale

Carn Vean

Mount
Todden

Battery &
Watch Hse

Mount
Todden
Down

Darrity's Hole

Normandy

Gap Point

Nature Trail

Normandy
Hotel

Normandy
Down

Lunnon

A3110

Deep
Point

Carn
Friars

Carn Friars Lane

Twin
Sisters

Higher Moors

Carn Friars
Farm

Water
Rocks

Porth Wreck

melethen

Hide

Horse
Rock

Cloudsley
Shovell
Monument

Porth
Hellick
Down

Sun
Rock

Jacky's Point

kee

Porth
Hellick

Loaded
Camel
Rock

Giant's Tomb Entrance Grave
Bronze Age C25th BC-C7th BC

Drum
Rock

Carn
Nore

Porth Hellick
Point

Pig Rock

Newfoundland Rocks

*Salakee
Down*

Porth
Loggos

Newfoundland Point

Church
Porth

Tom Butt's Bed

Cita wrecked 1998

Giant's Cliff Castle
Iron Age C7th BC - C1st AD

Church Point

Church Ledges

St Mary's

0		0.5		1km

0	1/4		1/2 mile

Age cultures of the Atlantic seaboard. Some of the most notable monuments are the exceptional Giant's Tomb on Porth Hellick Down, Innisidgen entrance grave on Helvear Down and Bant's Carn entrance grave on Halangy Down. Below Bant's Carn lies the later, more domestic scene of Halangy Down Iron Age village where you can wander around the 3,000 year old round houses.

When the low lying plain of the single prehistoric Isle of Ennor became submerged in about 1000AD St Mary's started to emerge as a separate island. The now demolished Ennor Castle at Old Town became the principal seat of Norman civil administration and Old Town itself became the major port on the islands.

Longrock Bronze Age menhir near Telegraph. There in another menhir on St Mary's near the daymark at Harry's Walls above Porthloo. Also see the Old Man on Gugh and the statue on Chapel Down, St Martin's.

The growth of sea trade from the Tudor period and the strategic position of Scilly on the new Atlantic trade routes to America and Africa brought the islands to the attention of national government. In order to safeguard its position fortifications were started. The first was Harry's Walls above Porth Mellon where the new theories of gunnery angles and arcs of fire were implemented in the design of the bastion wall. However the site was poorly chosen and it gave only limited protection to shipping at anchor in St Mary's Road. It was abandoned before it was completed in favour of batteries on the Garrison.

Elizabeth I consolidated the Garrison as a fortress by the building of the Star Castle. Hugh Town developed in the protective shadow of the castle during the C18th and C19th. The Garrison walls were progressively added in Elizabethan times until the whole headland was effectively fortified.

Reconstruction of an Iron Age Courtyard House.
Best examples - Nornour & Halangy Down Ancient Village.

St Mary's Island Walk

If you do not wish to walk the whole coast path you might decide to take the bus to the north end of the island and walk back to Hugh Town via Porth Hellick and Old Town. It would be worth taking a pasty or lunch with you to eat at Innisidgen or Watermill Cove. Best place to stop for a swim is Pelistry Bay.

Distance: *5 miles round trip (3-4 hours).* **Bus:** *Island bus service leaves from The Parade in Hugh Town.*
Pub/Refreshments: *Cafes at Porthloo, Old Town, Carn Vean & Hugh Town. Pubs in Hugh Town.*

> *Walk along the Strand following the road past the school & lifeboat house to Porth Mellon. Take the coast path above the beach to Harry's Walls.*

Mount Flagon & Harry's Walls

Abandoned soon after it was started in 1551 because it was poorly sited for the use of cannons. The builder had obviously not quite understood the principles behind the new weapon technology of the C16th. A Bronze Age menhir stands below the shipping daymark.

Halangy Down Ancient Settlement & Bant's Carn Entrance Grave

The entrance grave is one of the best examples on the islands and dates from the late Stone Age/early Bronze Age. The settlement of round houses and a single courtyard house are later, dating from the Iron Age. A booklet is available from the Custodian giving a detailed history and explanation of the site.

Innisidgen Entrance Graves

Another good Bronze Age entrance grave, perhaps as much as 4,500 years old.

Pelistry Bay & Toll's Island

Favourite beach for many on St Mary's and good place for a family day out. Beware of the tidal currents when the bar is covered. Toll's Island has the remains of Civil War gun platforms and on the south of the island a string of kelp pits used to burn seaweed to make soda and potash for the glass industry.

Porth Hellick Down

A concentration of entrance graves including the very large and fine example of the Giant's Tomb - the largest entrance grave on Scilly.

Old Town

Formerly *Porthennor* - the original Early Medieval settlement at a time when the present day islands were just starting to emerge from the single Isle of Ennor. Barely anything survives of the C13th Ennor Castle, the early Medieval administrative centre of the islands. It was demolished and robbed of stone when the Star Castle was constructed in the C16th. A Medieval pier is visible at low water as a curve of jumbled rocks and a Medieval granite trough sits nearby for salting and preserving fish.

> *Cafe at Old Town. If you would like to return to Hugh Town follow the road at the head of the beach.*

Peninnis Head

Popular place for an evening stroll. The granite has weathered into weird shapes. Look for the Pulpit Rock, The Monk's Cowl, Tooth Rock or make up your own names.

The Star Castle & Garrison

The Star Castle was started in 1593 in response to the failed Spanish Armada of 1588. It's part of a chain of similar castles that stretch along the English south coast from Deal in Kent to Pendennis Castle at Falmouth. The main coastal footpath follows the later C17th & C18th walls that further fortified the Garrison against attack. The walls are punctuated at intervals by bastions designed to house batteries of cannon to cover entry to the sheltered anchorage of St Mary's Road.

Tickets for inter-island boat service

Newman

Rat Island

Scillonia berth

Store House Battery

King Charles' Battery

Inter-isla boat ser

Pottery

Old pi

Barrel of Butter

The Star Castle

Tow Beac

Doctor's Keys

Hugh House

The Garrison

Hugh Town

Steval

Steval Point Battery

Steval Battery C19th

Garrison Farm

Brow Breeze

Por

Woolpack Battery C19th

Serica Rock

Morning Poi Battery

Woolpack Point

Woolpack Battery

Fenn

Wr

Woolpack

Big

The Bronze Age entrance Grave on Buzza Hill looking over Porthcressa and Hugh Town towards the Garrison

Canons have been reinstated at King Charles Battery. At Woolpack Point you can take a short cut back to Hugh Town by climbing up the hill to Woolpack C19th Coastal Defence Battery. One of a series of batteries around the British coast that were built in 1900 in response to political instability and revolution in Europe. The battery became redundant along with all coastal batteries with the invention of the atomic bomb in the 1950's. The TIC have a leaflet that covers this walk in great detail.

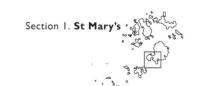

Peninnis Head

Peninnis Head is a favourite place for an evening stroll. The changing light brings out the many unusual shapes of the granite rock formations. The lighthouse was erected in 1911. It superseded the old lighthouse on St Agnes and marks the important entrance to St Mary's Sound. If you feel like extending the walk from Peninnis, follow the coast path to Old Town and return to Hugh Town via the footpath above the beach towards the school and Moor Well or take the nature trail across the Lower Moors to Porth Mellon.

The Garrison & Peninnis Head

Section 2.
St Agnes & Gugh

> **Food & Drink**
> St Agnes PO & Stores sells pasties and other provisions. The
> Turk's Head pub at Porth Conger is a popular eating place.
> Covean & Rose Cafes for tea and cakes.
>
> **Best things to do**
> Picnic on Periglis and look over to the Western Rocks & the
> Bishop Rock Lighthouse. Cove Vean about as perfect a beach
> as you will find - especially good for swimming.
>
> **Ferry**
> The ferry leaves from the quay at Porth Conger.

St Agnes and Gugh are the smallest and most self
contained of the inhabited islands. They are separated
from the rest of the group by the deep channel of St
Mary's Sound. St Mary's and the other inhabited islands
share the sheltered waters of The Road and Crow Sound
and were still joined together as recently as 600 years
ago. St Agnes has probably been a separate island for
1,000 years. The early separation from the other islands
has allowed St Agnes to retain a strong Celtic flavour. It
shares this with Samson and some of the more remote
corners of West Cornwall with their Celtic holy wells
and ancient superstitions and stories. In Celtic religion,
wells and springs where thought to be a special conduit
to the underworld - a sort of prehistoric cosmic
wormhole. When Christianity became the dominant
religion in the last centuries of the first millennium, the
early Christians absorbed and recycled elements of the
old religion. So the wells that once served for pagan
religion became 'holy' wells renamed after Christian
saints.

St Agnes has a fascinating example of this phenomenon
in St Warna's Well, on the west side of Wingletang Down.
The name Warna is unknown anywhere else as a Celtic
saint and the origin may belong to one of the many
savage Celtic water goddesses. Local tradition, dismissed
for many years, said that offerings thrown into the well
would 'ease' the passage of a ship onto the rocks. At one
time shipwrecks were a vital additional income and
resource for coastal communities. When the site was
excavated this century a number of ancient gold pins
were found at the bottom of the well. In fact St Agnes'
position as the first landfall on the prevailing westerly
winds has probably always given it a larger proportion
of shipwrecks than the other islands. But such was the
carnage in the C19th that the island had its own lifeboat
stationed at Periglis from 1890 to 1920. The crew
constituted 10% of population of the whole island. The
grand lighthouse in the centre of the island no longer
shows a light but it still serves as a daymark for shipping
and because it's visible from all parts of St Agnes acts as
a reference point for visitors. It was superseded by
Peninnis Head Lighthouse on St Mary's.

Everyone has their favourite beaches on Scilly, but in
Periglis, Cove Vean and The Bar, St Agnes has some of

St Agnes Lighthouse

the loveliest. Periglis stretches out into the Atlantic and one can sit here and watch the Western Rocks submerge and resurface with the tide. Sometimes it really does feel like the last beach in the world. The white flakes of mica in the sand stick to the skin like fish scales and young children playing in the sand take on the appearance of mermaids. An appropriately Celtic transformation in a tradition where many of the wind sculpted rocks are named after animals and appear to come alive in the swirling sea mists that drift in from the Atlantic.

Cove Vean is more sheltered and perfect for exploring the foreshore at low water. The best walk on St Agnes is down Barnaby's Lane. In the Spring it is an oasis of lush vegetation and flowers on this otherwise exposed island. The Turk's Head pub at Porth Conger is one of the islands greatest assets. Residents from St Mary's often make the trip in the Summer for a drink which can be considered something of a miracle, as they rarely visit the off-islands.

The Gugh

Gugh like Samson, its physical twin, is rich in archaeological remains. It forms the end of a chain of hills starting from Samson Hill on Bryher, and passing through Samson itself, which seem to have had a special importance for the prehistoric inhabitants of Scilly. All these hills have alignments of large and impressive entrance graves on their summits - a sort of Beverly Hills of the prehistoric dead. They may have had added significance as prehistoric burial places because of the views over the sea to the setting sun - views which still make them popular places today. Many of the entrance graves on the islands - not just the hilltop ones, are set in places with impressive views. It seems reasonable to speculate that this was one of the most important characteristics of a site to ancient people - after all it is still important to us 3,000 years later.

Gugh is linked to St Agnes at low water by a sand and shingle bar - be sure to know the tide times when you set off, because apart from being marooned on the island, there are strong currents over the bar at high water which would make it unsafe to swim back. In the Summer the neck of Gugh is covered in a thick blanket of impenetrable bracken but there is always a good path to Dropnose Porth, a popular sheltered place to swim, and up to the Old Man of Gugh an ancient standing

Round Rock of
Porth Coose

Little Smith
Browarth

Little Smith Brow

Porth Coose Carn

Barrel of Butter
Tins Walbert

Carn of
Porth Killier

*Porth
Coose*

Port
Killie

Three Brothers

Big
Pool

Burnt Island

Ginamoney
Carn

Big Carn

Carn of
Porth Killier

Fennel

Periglis

Little Carn

Lower To
Farm

Blanket
Bay

Old lifeboat slip

Mi
To

Gunner

*Lower
Town*

Peeresses
Middle Penny Ledge

Bergecooth

Bergecooth Carns

Tamerisk

Downs
Farm

②

Carns of Castella

Troy Town
Farm

Nag's Head

Garab

Carnew Point

Castella

Troy Town Maze
Prehistoric?/C17th

Carn Grigland

Carnew Rock

Down

Menglow

Beat
Carn

Pink
Carn

*St Warna's
Cove*

Camper Dizzle

Castle
Brose

Little
Castle
Vean

St Wa
Carn

Long Point

Castle
Vean

Great Porth Warna

HMS Firebrand wrecked 1707

Little Shoal
of Mackerel

Little Porth Warna

Little Porth As

Western Rock

Porth A

Ragged Rock

St Warna's Well
Iron Age?

Lethegus Rocks

Shooting Rock

Eastern Rock

*The B
Hor*

S M I T H   S O U N D

*Manx Shearwater.
Breeds on the neighbouring
uninhabited Isle of Annet.*

stone. The southern end of Gugh is inhabited by breeding gulls in the Summer and is best avoided - apart from the disturbance to the birds you are likely to find yourself being dive bombed by irate parents as you approach the nest sites. The gulls have an uncanny accuracy with their fishy faeces that discourages most intruders.

The present human inhabitants have been on the island since the 1940's, when they constructed the barns that overlook The Cove. Before that, Gugh had probably been uninhabited since the Iron Age, 1,500 years ago. In Spring Iron Age huts circles are visible at Tol Tuppens and on the north east side of Kittern Hill. An alignment of late Bronze Age entrance graves and cairns crown Kittern Hill - they are joined by a contemporary stone field wall. This association has led to speculation about a possible link between the monuments and fertility. One theory suggests that the entrance graves were built because of a crisis in food production caused by poor cultivation methods. This would certainly go some way to explaining

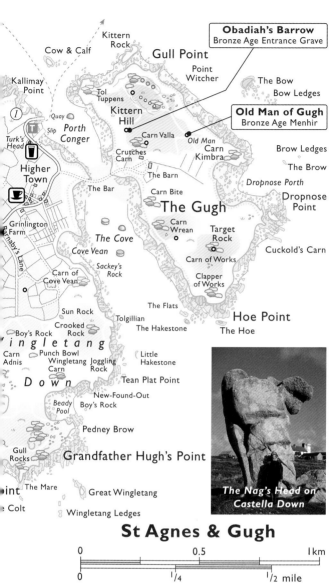

Obadiah's Barrow
Bronze Age Entrance Grave

Old Man of Gugh
Bronze Age Menhir

The Nag's Head on Castella Down

St Agnes & Gugh

the extraordinarily large number of ancient monuments on Scilly.

South east of Kittern Hill is the Old Man of Gugh, a Bronze Age menhir or standing stone. It has been standing here looking over what is now St Mary's Sound for the last 3,500 years. It is interesting to stand here and take a minute to think about how the landscape has changed since the stone was erected. When it was first put up, St Mary's Sound was probably a shallow cove sandwiched between the high land of the Garrison and Gugh. To the north lay a cultivated lowland plain with field walls and tree cover that stretched between all the existing islands. In 3,500 years time in AD5500, with the present rate of sea rise of about 3mm a year, the sea level will be about 10.5 metres higher than today. The waves will then be lapping at the base of the old man himself and both the Garrison and Peninnis Head will be islands in their own right. St Agnes will be a tiny island about one tenth of its present-day size.

St Agnes Island Walk

St Agnes is easily walked in a morning and has more packed into its small size than any other island. If you want to simply sit and enjoy the view then Periglis is the most popular beach (if its too windy - try Cove Vean).

Distance: 3 miles round trip (2 hours). **Going:** Generally easy. **Refreshments:** Turks Head, Covean & Rose cafes.

① From the quay walk towards the popular bird watching site of Big Pool.

Periglis & the old lifeboat station

From *Per*-cove and *eglos*-church. This was probably the site of an early Christian chapel. A lifeboat was first stationed here in 1890. The present lifeboat station was built in 1903 and faces the Western Rocks - the site of a large number of wrecks. Many bodies from the loss of the Association, Eagle, Firebrand and Romney were buried here in 1707.

Bergecooth

Note the unusually vivid brick red granite on the foreshore.

Castella Down

In 1707 HMS Firebrand finally floundered on Menglow Rock just offshore after first hitting the Gilstone reef.

Troy Town Maze

There is some doubt as to age of this small maze - it was reinstated by a lighthouse keeper in the C19th, but may be much older. Similar mazes are found in Scandinavia and the Vikings certainly landed on Scilly to rape and pillage. In the C12th Orkneyingar Saga the Vikings mention the easy pickings that were to be had on Scilly.

The Nag's Head

This area forms part of the same band of granite that makes up Peninnis Head on St Mary's because in both places the granite weathers into strange animalistic shapes.

② For a quick return to the post office and shop or if you need a cup of tea in a hurry, return to Downs & Middle Town by the track at the head of St Warna's Cove.

St Warna's Well

Tiny stone lined well dedicated to a pre Christian, presumably Celtic deity. It is said that in the past, islanders would drop offerings into the well to summon wrecks onto the shore when times were hard. When the site was excavated a number of gold pins and other votive offerings were found at the bottom of the well.

Wingletang Down

Most of the paths on the north of Wingletang Down lead to the huge loaf shaped rock called the Punchbowl. These large odd shaped rocks have a certain strange magnetism. There is almost always someone standing here just staring at the rock and you will probably find yourself doing exactly the same thing to no apparent end. In Cornwall in the C19th there were many such celebrity rocks, often popular sites for Sunday picnics. Unfortunately most have been quarried away.

Beady Pool

Ceramic beads from the wreck of a Venetian ship are sometimes washed onto the beach. Examples are on show at the Island Museum on St Mary's. Look out for the Yellow Horned Poppy at the head of the beach. Boy's rock was where the body of young lad was found.

Section 3.
The Western Rocks & The Bishop

Known to seafarers over the centuries as the *Dogs of Scilly* and the most notorious reef of rocks on the Western Approaches. They have witnessed hundreds of wrecks and claimed thousands of lives - reportedly over 2,000 in one night alone when part of the British fleet foundered here in 1707. The prevention of disastrous wrecks was not helped by a long standing error in nautical charts that showed the rocks 10 miles further north before 1750. Added to that was a poorly understood sea current that tended to push shipping further north than expected. Navigation in the days of sail was an imprecise science. A captain could easily establish his position along a north/south line - his latitude by reference to the pole star in its constant position overhead. What he could not do with any accuracy was establish his position on an east/west line - his longitude. If it was cloudy all he could do was dead reckon - make an informed guess of his position based in the assumed speed and direction of the vessel.

The shock of the loss of the British Fleet on the Western Rocks in 1707 spurred the Admiralty to set a prize for the first person to find a reliable method of establishing longitude. This was theoretically straightforward. If you knew the time of midday at your departure point, you could measure the disparity between that, and the time of midday at your present position. In this way, the number of hours, minutes and seconds could be translated into miles east/west of your starting point. In combination with your latitude this gave you an exact position. The theory was fine but the practice was very different. Clocks at this time were accurate on land but because they were pendulum clocks, they could not keep time on a ship that was pitching and rolling in the ocean. One man started to work towards a solution. He was John Harrison, the son of a Yorkshire carpenter and a master clockmaker. The rest of his life was spent working on a spring based mechanism that would be unaffected by the motion of a ship. This became known as Harrison's Chronometer and was the forerunner of the pocket watch.

Harrison eventually won the prize after a number of sea trials proved the accuracy of his chronometer.

The first Bishop Rock Lighthouse. Started in 1847 but washed away in 1850, before it could be commissioned.

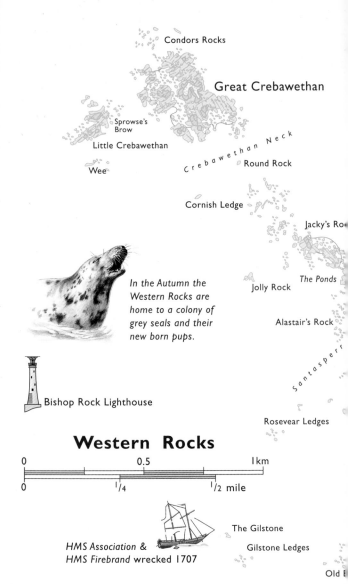

Condors Rocks

Great Crebawethan

Sprowse's Brow

Little Crebawethan

Crebawethan Neck

Wee

Round Rock

Cornish Ledge

Jacky's Ro

In the Autumn the Western Rocks are home to a colony of grey seals and their new born pups.

Jolly Rock

The Ponds

Alastair's Rock

Santasperr

Bishop Rock Lighthouse

Rosevear Ledges

Western Rocks

0	0.5	1 km

0	1/4	1/2 mile

HMS Association & HMS Firebrand wrecked 1707

The Gilstone

Gilstone Ledges

Old E

The wreck of the Association

Admiral Sir Cloudsley Shovell was one of the most celebrated sailors of his time. At the age of 15, during the Dutch War of 1665-7 he showed bravery that was to later become legendary by swimming between ships during a sea battle with battle orders in his mouth.

In 1707 the British fleet under Sir Cloudsley's command was returning from the Mediterranean where they had been fighting Barbary pirates. The fleet of 21 ships was hit by bad weather in the Bay of Biscay and became disorientated. Shovell called a meeting on his flagship HMS Association to try to reach agreement on their position. After much discussion they eventually agreed that they were well south of Scilly. Only one man dissented. He was a Scillonian by birth and said that he thought them to be only a few miles west of the islands.

Later that night the fleet struck the Western Rocks. Four ships went down in quick succession. The next day, Sir Cloudsley's body was washed ashore at Porth Hellick - still alive. He was said to have been murdered where he lay by a local woman who wanted to steal his ring. His body was buried at the head of the beach. It was later exhumed, pickled in brandy and laid to rest in Westminster Abbey.

24

The Bishop

The Bishop Rock has been performing the last rites on ships and crews ever since man first set sail in this part of the world. It is probably the most exposed of all the lighthouses around our coast. The rock itself is about 30 by 15 metres wide and is almost completely covered by a high Spring tide. It rises almost vertically from about 50 metres below sea level and so does not show the usual tell tale signs of breaking water that warn of a reef.

There are all number of explanations as to why the rock is called The Bishop. The most common is because of its similarity to the shape of a bishop's mitre. A more interesting one is that The Bishop and its near neighbour The Clerk, are named after two men found clinging to the rocks after a merchantman was wrecked here in C17th. The rocks were so isolated and little

Silver Carn

Rosevear

Old Blacksmith

evear Neck

Inner Rags

Rosevean

Rags

Shoal Neck

Gorregan

Carn Lawrance

Jenkin's Rocks

Carn Ithen

Broad Neck

Rosevean Neck

Dry Splat

Camperdown

Hole of Gorregan

Daisy

Trenemene

Black Rock

nathise Head

visited, that in those days the first indication of a wreck was often when bleached and bloated bodies started to wash ashore on St Agnes or at Porth Hellick on St Mary's. The threat to ships was so great that in 1680 one of the first lighthouses in Britain was constructed on St Agnes, but as it is 5 miles distant from the Bishop, and only had a weak light from a coal burning cresset, it was all but useless in fog and bad weather when it was most needed.

Fog Bell

The second Bishop Rock Lighthouse. Started in 1858 - severe storms caused the structure to shudder as waves passed over the top, shattering the 12cm thick glass windows and carrying away the half ton fog bell. Water poured into the lighthouse through the damaged lantern threatening to flood the inside and drown the keepers.

For many years the difficult engineering task of putting a lighthouse on the Bishop, in such an exposed position was insurmountable. A design was finally agreed in 1847 and a blacksmith shop was set up on Rosevear. It took three years to construct and work was abandoned each Winter and resumed in the following Spring.

Cast iron columns were used in the hope that waves would simply pass through the structure. Keepers gained access to the accommodation via a central column. The whole structure was tied to the rock with huge cast iron bolts. On February 5th 1850, a storm simply washed the lighthouse from its base before it had even been commissioned. Prospective lighthouse keepers could have been forgiven for becoming rather apprehensive at the thought of serving on the Bishop.

Work restarted in 1858, this time on a design using a solid tower structure constructed from carefully dovetailed blocks of Cornish granite. This lighthouse saved lives even before it was completed. Survivors of a wreck were found one morning sheltering in the partially completed structure by a group of surprised masons.

Lantern

Service Room

Engine Room

Bedroom

Living Room

Oil Room

Store Room

Entrance

Water
Tank

Original wall of
2nd lighthouse

After completion it became almost immediately apparent that this structure was not strong enough to resist the very large waves to which The Bishop is subjected. Cracks were soon snaking up the sides of the tower and vibrations caused by the waves passing over the lighthouse made it shake violently, knocking plates and pots off the shelves. Apparently once the keepers were able to watch fish swim past the kitchen window 25 metres up. In April 1874 waves in excess of 40 metres high broke clear over the tower, washing away the lantern and bringing tons of water into the lighthouse, threatening to drown the keepers.

In 1881 an outer stone skin was built around the existing tower increasing its height and strength. Since then the structure has been without problems. The last keeper left in 1992 when the lighthouse became fully automated.

The third Bishop Rock Lighthouse. An outer casing sheathed the second weakened lighthouse.

26

Section 4.
Samson

This small, now deserted island has an almost magical pull on many visitors and is often spoken of as the most vividly remembered part of any visit to the islands. It is a small but perfectly formed sensory masterpiece. Its twin hills and low lying neck form a neat figure of eight shape and give Samson a pleasing sense of serenity.

The concentration of prehistoric monuments on the twin hills suggest that it has been an important place since the islands were first settled in the Bronze Age and some archaeologists feel the settlement hidden beneath the sands of East Porth may have been one of the half dozen primary settlements in prehistoric times. At that time of course Samson was not an island, it was part of a much bigger single isle that took in almost all the present day islands. As the sea has submerged the land, the field walls that once penned in cattle in the Bronze

Bronze Age burial cist on Samson. Cists are usually found beneath a cairn or covering of stones. Evidence of cremated human bones have been found at a number of sites.

and Iron Age, were used to trap fish in the C19th. The fields now cross the sandbanks beneath the high tide. It was only 500 years ago that Samson was finally separated from Tresco and Bryher and even today on a low Spring tide in August it is perfectly possible to walk across the sands to Tresco and only get your knees wet (see photo on back cover).

Samson is part of a chain of hills that form the western rim of the islands. They run north to south from Shipman Head to Samson Hill on Bryher, through the twin hills of Samson to Kittern Hill on Gugh. Each hill in this series is crowned with the tombs of the first Scillonians. Its not hard to imagine the attraction of these places to the Bronze Age people - after all we are still attracted to them to watch the sun sink in the west on a Summers evening. The ancients must have had a heightened sensitivity to their environment because they lived in much closer and more dependent contact with the landscape than we do. In the later Celtic tradition the whole landscape was almost literally alive. It is perfectly possible that the twin hills were felt to represent the

Abandoned homes on the South Hill
of Samson looking north to Bryher and Tresco

breasts of a mother earth figure. This is a common
prehistoric interpretation of such topography and is found
in many ancient cultures. A modern day observer
glimpsing the setting sun between the twin paps
of Samson may even experience an ancient
stirring in their prehistoric heart.

About 30 years ago a stone lined grave
was uncovered on the foreshore of East
Porth. It was thought to be associated with   **White Islan**
the lost chapel of St Samson. Excavations
uncovered a timber structure thought to date
from about the C6th. Further north the foundations of
a later, rectangular stone building, two graves and a
possible stone font were discovered. The later structures
would appear to be contemporary with the early Christian
sites on St Helen's and Tean.

After a long period of being uninhabited Samson was
probably resettled after the Civil War and by the beginning
of the C19th about forty people were living here. They
seem to have lived in pretty dire circumstances subsisting
mostly on potatoes and limpets. Even today you can see
the large waste tips of limpet shells outside every house.
The island was really too small and its resources were
too poor to comfortably support a community. Water was
difficult to collect and there was no wood for fuel. The
islanders having to rely on collecting bracken and
driftwood from the shore. In the early part of the C19th
the island was hit by a series of droughts and by the time
Augustus Smith took on the lease of the islands in 1834
most of the inhabitants were destitute. Augustus Smith
provided housing on St Mary's for those that wanted to
move off the island and by 1855 the island was empty.

The picturesque decay of the abandoned homes
became an inspiration to the Romantic poet Tennyson
and for the Victorian novel *Armorel of Lyonnesse* by Sir
Walter Besant. Samson soon became a popular place to
picnic.

The wreck of HMS Colossus

The Colossus was returning home in November 1798
after being engaged in chasing Napoleon's fleet across
the Mediterranean throughout the previous Summer. She
took part in the Battle of Cape St Vincent and also in the
Battle of the Nile in which Lord Nelson destroyed
Napoleon's navy and thwarted

Yellow Rock

Little Rag Ledge

Puffin Island

Bollard Point

Great Rag Ledge

Channel Ledge

Landing Beach

Bar Point

North Hill
Entrance Graves
Submerged prehistoric field walls

Black Ledge

| **Prehistoric Burial Cists** |
| Bronze Age C25th BC-C7th BC |

East Par

SAMSON FLATS

West Par

The Neck

Site of Early Christian chapel

Well

| **Abandoned Houses** |
| C17th to C19th |

South Hill

hag oint

| **Entrance Graves** |
| Bronze Age C25th BC-C7th BC |

rbarrel Rock
Otto wrecked
1869 with a
argo of tar

Southward Well Point

Great Minalto Ledges

Southward Well

HMS Colossus wrecked 1798

Samson

| 0 | | 0.5 | | 1km |
| 0 | 1/4 | | 1/2 mile | |

his imperial ambitions. The Colossus was badly damaged in the encounter and after the battle retired to Naples for repairs and celebrations. The celebrations and the repairs were short lived. Napoleon's army was approaching Naples and Sir William Hamilton, the British representative to the Court of Naples was forced to evacuate but not before his wife Lady Emma's heart missed a beat when she met Nelson.

The Colossus was in poor shape, but she was forced to make her weary way under escort to Scilly where she anchored in St Mary's Sound. There followed a week of southerly gales that strained her already damaged fabric and eventually her main anchor cable parted and she was driven onto Southward Well reef. The crew was taken off by local boats but the ship was a complete loss along with Sir William's priceless second collection of Etruscan and Greek pottery (his first makes up the core of the British Museum's collection).

Section 5.
Bryher

Food & Drink
Bryher PO & Stores sells pasties and provisions. Hell Bay Hotel & Fraggle Rock have bar & restaurant. Vine Cafe serves tea & cakes.
Best things to do
Picnic on Gweal Hill & watch the sunset over the Norrard Rocks. Samson Hill has wonderful views.
Ferry
At low water ferries leave from the pontoon on the Bar. At high water ferries leave from Church Quay.
Ferry times and information on the boards at The Town & near the Hell Bay Hotel.

For many people Bryher is the most characteristic island of the whole group. On some days it can be almost frighteningly bleak as waves pile into Hell Bay, but then the next day it can be achingly beautiful and calm. In common with St Agnes the other sentinel on the western edge of the islands, Bryher gets a real bashing in the Winter months. It faces the full force of westerly storms and gales. The southern end is more sheltered part of the island and this is where all the present day inhabitants live. There is quite a marked division between the northern and southern parts of the island.

The northern end is a plateau of exposed high ground, sparsely covered in dwarfed and prostrate heather that hug the ground to avoid the desiccating winds that sweep across the downs. Shipman Head Down has an exceptional concentration of cairns - man made stone mounds usually built up over an ancient burial although some may simply be the result of land clearance. In the Bronze Age the climate was going through a mini heat wave which lasted some hundreds of years and areas which today seem exposed and waterlogged were then good agricultural land. Over one hundred cairns are still in existence here, many aligned or linked by low walls. Most have been greatly eroded over the last 3,000 years and at first it can be difficult to distinguish the man made cairns from the surrounding natural rock debris. However, the longer you look the more obvious the cairns become. When your eye is tuned in, you suddenly realise that you are walking in a Bronze Age cemetery where many generations of ancient Scillonians have been buried.

In storms the fetch of the waves that strike Bryher can be as much as 2,000 miles. As the waves arrive in the shallow water west of the island they are slowed by the rough seabed and pile up to a great size. Thousands of tons of water then drop on the coast with every breaker. In bad weather Hell Bay certainly lives up to its name - it becomes a furious caldron of foaming sea and in the worst storms waves will break clean over the top of Shipman Head. At such times the name of nearby Badplace Hill seems comically understated.

The extreme exposure of this part of the island, even within the terms of the Isles of Scilly gives it a sense of

▶ 32

Bryher Island Walk

The best views are from Watch Hill and Samson Hill. The beaches are the best on the eastern side of the island but can feel exposed on a windy day. Kitchen Porth is always more sheltered and has plenty of pools to explore at low water.

Distance: 4 miles round trip (2 hours).

Going: Generally easy along the south of the island. The northern end at Shipman Head Down & Badplace Hill is a little more difficult.

① *From Church Quay walk a few metres along the road and turn left through a small gap in the sand dunes and onto Green Bay beach.*

Green Bay prehistoric field walls

About half way along the beach you will come across a line of large stones disappearing into the water. This is all that remains of a Bronze Age field boundary that has been swamped by the rise in sea levels in the last 3,000 years.

Continue towards the large bulk of Samson Hill.

Samson Hill

Great views to the south and west from the summit. Topped by a number of Bronze Age entrance graves. The best one is on the southern slope of the hill facing Samson.

Great Par

Here a gig shed has been converted into a gallery. The Hell Bay Hotel serves lunches

Great Pool & Gweal Hill

Gweal Hill is great place to watch the sun set over the Western and Norrard Rocks.

② *If you want to return to the east side of the island use the footpath that runs inland from Great Popplestone under Puckie's Carn. To continue the round island walk follow the coastal path.*

Shipman Head Down

On the surface of the down are an almost unprecedented concentration of cairns - prehistoric burial mounds.

Cliff Castle & Badplace Hill

You may be able to just make out the remains of a bank and ditch across the neck of the headland. The area was used as a cliff castle from the Iron Age. It also probably served as a temporary refuge from Viking marauders in the early Medieval period.

It is possible to cross the Gulf to Shipman Head via the neck of slippery rocks. Watch the tide though or you will be marooned on the House of the Head.

Shipman Head

Beyond the shelter of Scilly Rock and the Norrard Rocks this headland takes the full brunt of Atlantic storms. Waves break over the top in severe storms.

Hangman's Island & Kitchen Porth

Hangman's island is said to have been used to hang mutinous sailors. The jib is modern.

The Bar

Main landing place at low water when Church Quay dries out. Before the construction of the pontoon passengers used to have to walk the plank from the bow of the boat onto the sand. The new pontoon was built as part of the Challenge Anneka television series.

Norrard and Kitchen Porth

House
the H

foreboding even on a calm day. Below Badplace Hill are the remnants of defensive earthworks that formed the landward defensives of Shipman Head Cliff Castle. The headland was fortified in the Iron Age presumably to provide short term shelter to islanders from marauding Irish raiders. The House of the Head cannot help but bring to mind the Iron Age Celts and their cult of head worship. Severed heads were sometimes used to decorate their homes. It always sends a tingle running through my neck.

Horse Rock

Poppleston
Brov

P o p p l e s t o n e   N

Gweal

Black
Carn

G w e a l   N e c k

Camper

Gw
H

Wether
Carn

Gweal Ledges

Crow Island

Stinking Po

Merrick Island

Moon Rock

Trueb
Rock
Stor

Touch Rock

Gulf Rock

The Gulf

Riceman's Hole

Gerwick
Ledges

Droppy N
Point

Gerwick

Shee
Ledg

N e c k   o f   G e r

The southern part of Bryher is protected from the storms by the Norrard Rocks and here there are large sweeping bays backed by sand dunes often punctuated by huge loaf shaped granite outcrops such as Great Carn which children can never resist clambering over. This part of Bryher sometimes seems to be more beach than island. At the very southern tip of the island is the impressive bulk of Samson Hill attached to the rest of Bryher by a low lying sandy neck. It gives the appearance of having been tacked on to the end of Bryher almost as an afterthought. It is as if it had broken away from Samson and slowly drifted north to strand itself on the beaches of Bryher. The hilltop is crowned with two fine entrance graves and there are great views over to the Western and Norrard Rocks. It is especially worth coming up here in the evenings as the sun sets in the west. Below Samson Hill are the lovely intimate bays of Great Porth and Stony Porth.

A prehistoric boundary wall survives on the beach of Green Bay - the large seaweed covered boulders marching into the sea and across the sand flats.

New Grimsby Sound

hipman Head

Kettle

Kettle Point

Gun Hole

Little Kettle

Cork Porth

Piper's Hole

Gun Hill

Gun Well

Gimble Point

Tregarthen Hill

King Charles' Castle

Tresco

the Gulf

Smith's Hole

Hole of the Horse

Badplace Hill

Boat Carn

The Horse

Small Boat Carn

Pollock Rock

Cromwell's Castle

Castle Down

Great ussel Rock

ll Bay

Great Bottom

Gt. Bottom Carn

The Bight

Bight Drang

Bight Carn

Frenchman's Point

Anchor Drang

pman Head Well Dran

Anchor Carn

Hangman Island

New Grimsby Harbour

Braiden Rock

Cave

Prehistoric Cairns
Bronze Age

Shipman Head Down

Gt. Rock

Puckie's Carn

Kitchen Porth

Dunstan's Rock

Norrard

Watch Hill

Anneka's Quay (low water)

The Bar

Little oplestone

The Town

Vine Farm

Queen's Ledge

Halftide Bar

Great oplestone

New Road

Broomfield Carn

Church Quay (high water)

Plumb Island

Little Pool

Southward

Timmy's Hill

Merrick Island

Prehistoric Wall
Bronze Age

Plumb Rocks

Great Pool

Hell Bay Hotel

Community Centre

Hillside Farm

Veronica Farm

Green Bay

arn Bars

Gallery

The Green

Three Brothers

Point of Bars

Great Par

Great Carn

Brow Ledges

The Brow

Great Crabs Ledge

Little Crabs Ledge

Heathy Hill

Western Carn

Samson Hill

Lubber's Rock

ny Porth

Merrick Island

Rushy Bay

Bonfire Carn

Works Carn

Entrance Graves
Bronze Age C25th BC-C7th BC

's Rock

Stony th

George's Rock

Works Point

Great Rushy Bay Ledge

Middle Colvel Rock

Outer Colvel Rock

Yellow Rock

Little Rag Ledge

Puffin Island

Great Rag Ledge

Bollard Point

Landing Beach

amson

Bryher

0   0.5   1 km

¼   ½ mile

oo *Entrance Graves*

Section 6.
Tresco

Food & Drink
Quay Shop & cafe is renowned for its home made cakes.
Island Hotel has snacks & afternoon teas for visitors. New
Inn also serves food. Tresco stores has wide variety of food
and drinks.

Best things to do
Visit the Abbey Gardens and the shipwrecked figureheads at
Valhalla. Bike hire is available from the Estate Office.

Ferry
Most ferries will come into New Grimsby if they can. At low
water visitors from St Mary's will be landed at Carn Near
Quay on the southern tip of Tresco. Occasionally boats work
out of Old Grimsby. Ferry times & information on the boards
at Timothy's Corner & at Old Grimsby.

Tresco is leased from the Duchy of Cornwall by the
Dorrien-Smith family who live in Tresco Abbey. It is the
only island on Scilly that retains this old relationship
that once saw the whole group leased firstly, to the
Godolphin family and then in the C19th to Augustus
Smith. As proprietor of the islands, his humane and far
sighted approach revitalised the poverty struck islands.
He introduced new agricultural methods and developed
the flower and tourism industries. Emphasis was placed
on the importance of education for the children of Scilly
and he funded the building of schools on the islands. It
was Augustus Smith who started the Abbey Gardens -
now famous throughout the world for their sub-tropical
plants and beautiful setting.

Tresco Abbey has its origins in the C12th. Henry I
granted all the religious establishments on northern Scilly
(they were then one single isle) to the Benedictine monks
of Tavistock Abbey. The Abbey - properly a priory was
dedicated to St Nicholas. Gauging from the fragmentary
remains of the priory church it was a substantial building
by Scillonian standards, although it was probably home
to only a handful of monks at any one time. Scilly was
very vulnerable to raids by pirates and Vikings. The priory
and chapels would have been especially tempting targets.
In the Viking Orkneyinga saga Scilly is mentioned as an
easy target and details of a raid are recounted. The monks
didn't take it all lying down though, they had their own
zero tolerance policy. In 1209 they are supposed to have
beheaded 120 pirates in one afternoon. It was probably
a rare victory and the monks finally abandoned Tresco
in the C14th after about 300 years of occupation.

The remains of the church now form the framework
for one of the most delightful gardens in the country. In
common with many gardens in Cornwall the Abbey
Gardens are at their best in the Spring and early Summer.
The whole garden is protected by a belt of trees that
were originally planted by Augustus Smith - up to that
point there were no trees growing on Tresco. Many of
these trees were blown down in a series of storms that
culminated in the hurricane of 1990. Since then over

60,000 replacement trees have be planted to reestablish the shelter belt. Many of the original plants were purchased from passing sailing ships returning to Britain from the southern hemisphere. The beautiful blue Agapanthus are native to South Africa and the Echeiums are more commonly found in the Canary Isles.

The Abbey Gardens are also of interest to the non gardener because amongst the shrubs are a number of interesting artifacts gathered from the surrounding islands. The most ancient is a Bronze Age holed stone or menhir. There is a Romano-British inscribed stone and most interestingly, a Roman shrine found in a well beneath the Garrison wall. The side panels of the shrine have carved reliefs of a dagger and an axe indicting that it was probably a sacrificial altar. With the shrine at Nornour on the Eastern Isles this suggests Scilly was on a Roman trade route. At Valhalla there is a collection of figureheads from ships wrecked on the islands plus the brazier that was used to illuminate the old lighthouse on St Agnes.

There is plenty to see on the rest of the island after a visit to the gardens. The south of Tresco is covered with softly undulating sand dunes that are cloaked with wild flowers in the Spring and Summer. North of a line drawn between Old Grimsby and New Grimsby are the exposed cliffs of Castle Down.

New Grimsby Harbour is a favoured anchorage on Scilly and yachts often moor here in the Summer. In the days of sail ships it was the preferred anchorage in the islands because its protected from gales by the high ground on either side and has good holding ground for anchors. It is quite a confined space for a sailing ship and getting in and out could be a problem if the wind was light or from the wrong quarter. There are giant iron rings fixed to the rocks at the mouth of the Sound and these were used to pull and steady ships as they entered or left the harbour. King Charles' Castle was built on Castle Down in 1550 to protect the haven from the threat of invasion by the French and Spanish. At the same time the Blockhouse was built to protect Old Grimsby Sound and the deep water St Helen's Pool.

After the end of the English Civil War in 1648 Scilly took part in an uprising against Parliament and for a time the islands became a base for privateers and pirates. This so upset the Dutch that they declared war on the islands and sent a fleet of ships under Admiral Van Tomp to take the islands. Fearful that the islands would fall to a foreign power, Parliament sent its own force under Admiral Blake to subdue the rebels and defend the islands. He landed on the north of Tresco and set up defences at Oliver's Battery at Carn Near halting the resupply of the Star Castle which soon capitulated. King Charles' Castle was then replaced in 1651 by Cromwell's Castle. This was better sited at sea level in order to deter enemy shipping from entering New Grimsby Sound.

Tregarthen Hill
Bronze Age Entrance Grave

Kettle

Cork Porth

Piper's Hole (cave)

Old Grimsby Sound

Kettle Point

Gun Hole

Gun Hill

Gun Well

Tin prospecting pits

Tregarthen Hill

Castle Down Brow

Little Kittern

Gimble Point

King Charles' Castle

② ▯

Pollock Rock

Cromwell's Castle ▯

Castle Porth

Frenchman's Point

N o r t h   E n d

C a s t l e   D o w n

Beacon Hill

Old Lookout

Gimble Porth

Gimble Point

Merchant's Rock

Mercha Point

Isl H

Norrard

Hangman Island ⚑

Kitchen Porth

Braiden Rock

Dial Rocks

Back Lane

Townshill

Sch Comm Cen

New Grimsby Harbour

☕ ✉

Dunstan's Rock

Anneka's Quay (low water)

① Ⓣ ☕

Point Carn

The Palace Gallery

New Ing

Dolphin House

Dol Town

Watch Hill ☕

The Bar

New Grimsby

Timothy's Corner

Vane Hill

Racket Carn

Broomfield Carn

Church Quay (high water) Ⓣ

Green Bay

Merrick Island

Bryher

Brow Ledges

The Brow

Great Crabs Ledge

Little Crabs Ledge

Lubber's Rock

The Warren

Cliff Cottage

Old Seaplane Slip

Farm Beach

Estate Office

✉

Abbey Farm

Sluice Gate

Saffron Cove

Plumb Island

Plumb Rocks

Plumb Hill

Bay Row

Racket Tow Lane

Bird

Bird Hide

Abbey Drive

Abbey W

Samson Hill

Bonfire Carn

George's Rock

Works Point

Appletree Point

Appletree Carn

Abbey Hill

Apple Ban

Appletree Bay

R B

Little Rag Ledge ♦

Chinks

Puffin Island

Great Rag Ledge

Carn Ne Oliv Batt

Channel Ledge

Bar Point

Hulman

36

Cromwell's Castle

Northwethel

al
th

Round Rk.

en's
ock

Crow's
Island

Higher
Ledge

Middle
Ledge

Peashopper
Island

th Mellin Carn

Long Point

Hedge Rock

n's
h
Quay

Tide
Rock

Hedge Rock
Ledge

Old Grimsby

y Island

Lump of Clay
Ledge

Little Cheese
Rock

en Porth

Block House Point

Chinks

Block House
C16th Fortification

Blockhouse
Cottages

Cradle Point

Great Cheese
Rock

Rushy Point

Borough Road

Tea Ledge

Borough
Farm

Channel Rocks

Middle Down

Lizard Point

Parting
Carn

Lower
Scattering Rocks

Pool Road

at Pool

Pentle
House

Rowesfield
Cottage

Pentle Bay

Great Pentle
Rock

Little Pentle
Rock

Penzance Road

Tresco Abbey

Abbey Pool

Submerged
prehistoric
field walls

Skirt Island

y Green

Diamond
Ledge

Great Rock

Figtree
Rocks

Crab's Ledge

Bounty Ledge

Green Island

Tobaccoman's
Ledge

Sea Carn

Bathinghouse
Porth

Tobaccoman's Point

Submerged
prehistoric
field walls

Broad Ledge

Carn Near Quay
(low water landing)

Tresco

w Point

0   0.5   1km

0   1/4   1/2 mile

Tresco Island Walk

The northern part of the island is wild and exposed. The southern part of the island is almost all beach and dunes with the Abbey Gardens nestling in the centre.

Distance: 5 miles round trip for the whole island circuit (about 3¹/₂ hours). **Going:** Generally easy along south of the island - can also be walked along the beach at low water. The more rugged northern end of the island is a more typical cliff path walk. **Pub/Refreshments:** Pub lunch at New Inn. Cafe at New Grimsby Quay and refreshments from the Abbey Gardens (entrance fee) & Island Hotel.

① From the quay at New Grimsby follow the cliff path north towards Cromwell's Castle.

Cromwell's Castle

Until the Medieval period New Grimsby Sound was the main anchorage in the islands. The castle was constructed in 1651 to guard the main approach.

② Follow the footpath that runs up the hill immediately above Cromwell's Castle.

King Charles' Castle

Built before Cromwell's Castle in 1550, but was poorly sited and eventually superseded by Cromwell's Castle. Associated with extensive defensive groundworks which have been reinstated in recent years.

Follow the path towards Gun Hill.

Piper's Hole

Large cave with an internal pool that goes back 50 metres into the cliffs.

Tregarthen Hill

Fine entrance grave on the southern side of the summit. There are views over to Round Island and St Martin's and its a good spot to take a picnic.

The Island Hotel serves cream teas and bar meals.

Blockhouse

Built to protect the anchorage of St Helen's Pool in 1554 at the same time as King Charles' Castle and held by the Royalists during the English Civil War.

You can shortcut back to New Grimsby via Racket Town Lane.

Pentle Bay & Bathinghouse Porth

A number of submerged prehistoric hut circles and boundary walls are sometimes evident on the foreshore at Pentle Bay and Bathinghouse Porth - see map. Look out for the straight alignment of the boundary walls among the other boulders on the foreshore. The layer of peat that shows in the intertidal zone is evidence of the submergence of fields. You can sometimes see the remains of hut circles at Bathinghouse Porth but this is dependent on the level of sand cover.

You can shortcut back to New Grimsby via Pool Lane.

Abbey Farm

The buildings and slip here were established as a base for flying boats in both the World War I & II. Their principal tasks were to hunt down U-Boats prowling the Western Approaches and rescue downed pilots. The slip still survives on the foreshore.

The New Inn is just up from the beach at New Grimsby.

Section 7.
Tean, St Helen's & Round Island

All the islands in this northern part of Scilly are now uninhabited but were once home to at least two Celtic Christian saints. Inter-island ferries do not make regular landings here but will make special trips on request.

Tean (pronounced Tee-an)

This small island is the site of an Iron Age settlement and an early C8th Christian chapel. Hut circles and ancient field walls have been identified in the sandy bays of East and West Porth and in St Helen's Porth. Great Hill has an entrance grave as does the Old Man. The most well known site is St Theona's Chapel. When the site was excavated sixteen early Christian graves were found under the east wall of the small rectangular stone chapel. This showed the chapel to be from a later period than the earliest graves. They were probably dug at a time when the original wooden chapel was still standing over 1,000 years ago. It is thought that the graves are those of the founders of the site - one of which is the grave of St Theona herself. Unfortunately very little if anything is known of St Theona. It is assumed that Theona was a woman - and certainly women saints are common in the Celtic nations. The site must have been occupied at the same time as St Elidius's chapel on St Helen's (the islands were not separate at that point) and there were probably similar chapels on Samson, St Martin's and St Agnes.

St Helen's

The name St Helen's is actually a corruption of St Elidius who was an obscure Celtic saint. The remains of an early Christian Chapel and circular hermit cell are thought to date from the C8th. A similar structure has been uncovered at Perranporth in north Cornwall and many of the established churches in Cornwall probably started in the same way as St Elidius' chapel. Of Elidius we know little, except that he was said to be the son of a British king and a bishop in the early church.

St Elidius may have lived in the small circular cell. The site seems to have kept growing in religious importance and in the C11th about 300 years after the death of Elidius, a small church was built. At the same time a number of smaller rectangular buildings were constructed. They presumably housed the men and women who cared for the site. Inside the chapel is an altar with a hidden recess for holy relics of Elidius and a grave in the church is thought to belong to the man himself. The church was extended and embellished probably by the monks of Tavistock Abbey soon after they settled on Tresco in the C12th. The site fell into disuse and ruin in the C14th or C15th. A service is still held on the island on August 6th each year to celebrate the feast day of St Elidius. A display board at the site gives a detailed history of the ruins and has pictures of some of the artifacts found during the excavations. They are now housed in the Island Museum in Hugh Town on St Mary's.

On the southern side of the island lies a ruined

rectangular building. It is usually referred to as the *Pest House* and is an C18th isolation building used to quarantine sailors landed from disease ridden ships. It continued the St Helen's tradition for hermits and isolation but in this case it was enforced isolation.

To the west of the island lies a wide reef called the Golden Ball Brow which has claimed numerous ships. Its last victim was the Panamanian ship *Mando* in January 1955. When wind and tide conditions are right surfers sometimes wait here for the freak waves that occasionally hit the reef.

Men-a-vaur

Men-a vaur is in fact three separate rocks that rise suddenly and vertically out of the sea. It is said to be possible to sail a small dinghy between the walls of the rocks on a calm day and it became something of a rite of passage for local youngsters to attempt the feat. Puffins and guillemots nest on the sheer sides of the rock.

Tean, St Helen's & Round Island

40

Round Island from Tresco

Round Island

The lighthouse was built in 1887 and completed a ring of lighthouses that mark the Isles of Scilly from all parts of the compass. Its height of almost 70 metres above sea level often allows the light to be seen from the Land's End Peninsula, almost 30 miles away. The lighthouse is now automated as are all the lights around Scilly and Lands End. The island stands right on the edge of deep water and waves pile up as they suddenly hit the shallows. A storm in 1886 was found to have washed limpets and stones on to the roof of the accommodation building 60 metres above sea level.

Section 8.
St Martin's & The Eastern Isles

Food & Drink
Post Office & shop at Higher Town. St Martin's Hotel restaurant
for evening meals. Cafe in Higher Town. Seven Stones Inn
at Lower Town.

Best things to do
Explore Chapel Down. Good views from Cruther's Hill over
Crow Bar to St Mary's & from Chapel Brow to the Sevenstones
reef.

Ferry
Most ferries will call at both Higher Town and Lower Town
quays. At low water boats tend to come into the quay at
Lower Town.

St Martin's makes up the north eastern limit of Scilly and
is the most picturesque of all the islands. Seen from the
air it forms a distinctive crescent shape, with a spine of
high ground that curves along the centre of the whole
island from Chapel Down in the east, to White Island in
the north. More than any other island in the group St
Martin's is an island of sweeping bays. Almost all of the
cultivated land runs down from the spine of the island
to the south and western coasts that overlook Crow Sound
and the sand banks of St Martin's Flats. This side of the
island with its sunny aspect is covered with tiny sheltered
flower and vegetable fields. Wild Agapanthus, Lily and
Hottentot Fig grow from every hedge and wall and dunes
run down to the waterside, softening the whole coastline.
The sheltered, lush scallop shaped bays of Higher Town
and Lawrance's Bay run down to soft dunes.

The northeast side of the island makes a nice contrast
especially the magnificent St Martin's Bay. This side of
the island in uncultivated, weather beaten, wind blasted
and exposed - a bulwark to the North Atlantic.

The islanders' forefathers showed commendable
brevity in naming the three main settlements as Higher,
Middle and Lower Town. This no nonsense attitude to
place-names is a delightful understatement that could
only work on Scilly. It's a practice that St Martin's also
shares with St Agnes, the most south westerly island of
the group.

There are many good archaeological sites on the
island. A Bronze Age statue menhir has been repositioned
on the south of Chapel Down. The face is now ill defined,
but in the right sort of oblique light its features can be
made out but this is tricky unless you catch the sun in
exactly the right position. If you really want to see the
facial features it is best go up at night with a torch to
shine across the face perhaps then continuing to St
Martin's Head to watch the eight lighthouses whose lights
are visible from here. An alignment of entrance graves
crowns Cruther's Hill and echo similar groupings on the
western rim of the islands at Gugh and Samson.

Further northwest, there is a entrance grave on
Knackyboy Carn. There is not much to see now, but it
was excavated in the 1950's and found to be almost

▶ 44

St Martin's Island Walk

The island is split into two parallel and curved strips. The south and west facing coasts are cultivated and easy to walk. The north and west coast are more wild and bleak and are slightly harder going.

Distance: A complete circuit of the islands is about 6 miles (3 hours). If you don't want to do the whole circuit stroll up to Chapel Down & then walk back across the spine of the island. **Going:** Generally easy on the south of the island.
Pub/Refreshments: Sevenstones Pub at Lower Town. Tea & cakes at Higher Town & at St Martin's Hotel.

From Higher Town Quay follow the coast path over the dunes towards English Island Point.

Chapel Down Menhir

In the middle of a cairn above Carn Wethers is a small menhir or standing stone. There is a barely recognizable face carved into the stone. The features are much more apparent when the light falls obliquely on the face, or alternatively take a torch up at dusk.

St Martin's Head Daymark & Chapel

The daymark was erected in the C17th. The rectangular buildings are the remains of a Napoleonic signal station. Messages were relayed to ships off shore by semaphore. Below the daymark and usually obscured by vegetation, are the scant remains of an early Christian chapel. It was probably an early lighthouse run by a religious order. Look northeast and you may see waves breaking over the Sevenstones Reef - the grave of the Torrey Canyon in 1967.

Frenchman's Graves

Said to be the burial ground of a whole ship's crew wrecked on the rocks below. Cliff burial was common practice in the C17th and C18th for bodies washed ashore after a wreck. It was especially true for those thought to be the bodies of Frenchmen who had the temerity to be at the same time Catholic, Republican & French - not a popular recipe at the time.

Burnt Hill Cliff Castle

Thought to be the remains of a minor cliff castle or settlement from the Iron Age. The promontory is protected by low wall on the landward side. The outline of two round houses can just be made out inside the enclosure.

White Island

Accessible at low water only. The very northern tip of the island is composed of the only remnant of slate rock on Scilly. A fine entrance grave sits on the high ground to the north of the island and there is a good example of a kelp pit sitting just above the beach at Porth Morran.

Cruther's Hill

At the summit there is an alignment of entrance graves. Good view back towards Tresco and St Mary's over Crow Bar. At the time the entrance graves were constructed, they would have looked over fields and woods and not over sea as today. The people whose remains were deposited in the tombs probably farmed this now submerged land.

Knackyboy Carn

Just behind the carn are the remains of an excavated entrance grave which revealed a series of pottery urns filled with cremated human remains.

undisturbed by grave robbers. Seventy pottery urns were found in the chamber. They contained cremated bones and amber beads and brooches. It is unusual to find a tomb that has not been robbed of its contents.

An early Christian chapel once stood below the daymark on Chapel Down the rectangular foundations are visible early in the season before the bracken smothers them. It was probably built to show a light to guide shipping in the early Medieval period. It was common practice for religious houses to set up lights on the highest headlands often manned only by a solitary monk. Almost

Lion Rock
Brewer
Baker
West Withian
Shag Point
White Island
Entrance Grave
Cairns
Stony Porth
East With
Pernagie Isle
Round Rock
Porth Morran Quay
Kelp Pit
Camper Porth
Camper Po
Pernagie Brow
Pernagie Rock
Porth Morran
Chad Girt
Plumb Island
Butter Porth
Rushy Carn
Jacky's Poin
Round Bowl
White Island Bar
The Cove
Great Me Ledge
Rabbit Rocks
Scilly Point
Pernagie Point
Entrance Grave
Top Rock
Porth Seal
Top Rock Hill
Little Bay
Tean Sound
Little Merrick Led
Goat's Point
Tinkler's Rock
Tinkler's Hill
Sheep Ledge
St Martin's Hotel
Old Lookout
Seven Stones Inn
Great
Bab's Carn
Ashvale Farm
Middle Town
Frenchman's Graves
Lower Town
Lower Town/ Hotel Quay (low water)
Southward Carn
Neck of the Pool
Yellow Rock Carn
Knackyboy Carn
John Martin's Ledge
Yellow Rock
Jack's Ledge
School Lane
Chu Far
Dog Ledge
Round Rock Ledge
Lawrance's Brow
Polrea
Carrion Rocks
West Broad Ledge
Stephen's Ledge
Lawrance's Bay
Carron Farm
S T   M A R T I N ' S   F L A T S
Cruther's H
Moths Ledge
Old Quay
Pigs Ledge
Entrance Graves
Bronze Age
Crows Ne
Ho
Broad Ledge
Rc
Wra Ledge
Law

St Martin's

0   0.5   1 km

0   ¼   ½ mile

all the prominent headlands in Britain are named after a saint for this reason. The chapel was robbed of stone during the construction of the daymark and Napoleonic signal station that stand on Chapel Brow. The signal station used a semaphore system to communicate with naval vessels standing offshore ready to pounce on any passing 'Frenchie'. It was replaced after only a few years service by a purpose built tower at Telegraph on St Mary's.

It is worth a scramble across the rocks for a visit to White Island. The only slate rock on the otherwise granite islands is on the extreme north of the island. It is the only remnant of sediment from the Laurasian Mountains that once stood 5 miles high above the granite. The presence of the granite is an indication that a collision of continental plates took place to the south. The suture line between the plates runs along the line of the English Channel.

An entrance grave lies on the north of the island and

Tearing Ledges

ackerel Rocks   St Martin's Bay

Santamana Ledges

Signal Station
Napoleonic

Cliff Castle?
Iron Age

St Martin's Head

Murr Rock

Turfy Hill Point

Popplestone Corner   Daymark

Chapel Brow

N'ward Bight

Bull's Porth

Bread & Cheese Cove

Treweeke's Island   Burnt Hill   Stony Porth

Carn Leve'eth

S'ward Bight

C h a p e l   D o w n

Culver Hole

Cairns   Cairn & Menhir

Entrance Grave

Mullet Pool

Carn Wethers

Little Arthur Farm

May's Hill   John Batty's Hill

Middle Bight

arn

Brandy Point

her Town

Gun Hill   Perpitch

ool reen

English Island Carn

Statue Menhir?
Bronze Age C25th BC-C7th BC

Higher Town Quay (high water)

Higher Town Bay

English Island Point

her's Point   English Island   ENGLISH ISLAND NECK   **Nornour**

Settlement & Shrine
Romano-British C1st-C5th

a kelp pit sits just above the beach at Porth Morran. In the C17th and C18th a family from Falmouth called Nance started a cottage industry cutting seaweed to turn into kelp. The seaweed was cut, dried on the shore then burnt in the shallow stone lined pits to produce a dark green mass of kelp. Soda and potash were then extracted for use in the glass and soap industries. The end product gave old glass its characteristic green hue. This was a widespread industry on the western seaboard of Britain.

The process gave off copious amounts of noxious smoke and was unpopular with many of the inhabitants of the islands. It was never anything but a subsistence industry - but it was a period when island incomes were very low and poverty was rife. It took about 20 tons of seaweed (principally oar weed) to produce just one ton of kelp and must have been backbreaking work.

The Eastern Isles

A collection of small uninhabited and sheltered islands south of St Martin's. They are a favourite place for seals who haul themselves onto the rocks to bask in the sun. Grey seals spend most of their lives at sea but come inshore to moult and breed on the Eastern Isles. September and October are the main breeding months. The cows are able to give an exceptionally rich milk that allows the pups to gain 9 kilos in the first week after birth. After three weeks the pup is abruptly deserted by its mother and over the next two weeks and it lives off it's fat while the sea coat grows. At this time the cows will mate again but the fertilised egg will be not develop until the Spring. The bulls are more conspicuous than the cows because of their darker coats and larger size. The seals return in January and February to moult and allow their new sea coats to grow. These islands are covered by bracken from mid Summer onwards, so those wishing to see the archaeological remains should try to get to the isles in the first part of the year. Just above the beach on Nornour is a settlement of Iron Age courtyard houses - a more elaborate form of roundhouse with workrooms and store rooms around the sides of an open courtyard (see illustration on page 14). Nornour is a significant settlement in the history of the islands. It was founded in the Bronze Age but during the Roman period was expanded and may have been used as a shrine by mariners. Hundreds of fine brooches, pins, glass beads and jewellery have been

English Isl.

Inner Scud

Western Scud

Long Scud

Great Ganinick

Eastward Guthern

Great Ledge

Arthur Neck

Ganinick Brow

Cadedna Ledges

Little Ganinick

Higher Town Bay, St Martin's. Looking over to Cruther's Hill with its alignment of entrance graves on the summit. An absolutely characteristic site for Bronze Age entrance graves and similar to sites on Samson, St Agnes and Gugh.

found here along with Roman coins and other religious offerings. It may have also been the site of the main harbour on the islands in the Roman period. Another important find is a clay figurine, probably of the Roman goddess Venus. Finds from Nornour are exhibited in the museum on St Mary's.

On the foreshore of Nornour are the rusting boilers of the passenger paddle steamer Earl of Aran. In July 1862, she hit Irishman's Ledge just east of Nornour after the captain took the advice of a local man to take a short cut to St Mary's through English Island Neck. Woops.

Grey Seal

Settlement & Shrine
Romano-British C1st-C5th

Hanjague

glish Island Neck

sh Nornour
e

Irishman's Ledge

Nornour
Brow

Shag Rocks

Northward
Head

Round Rock

Aran wrecked
er shows at low
water

Jolly Point

Mouls

Holmbush Carn

Great Ganilly

Little
Innisvouls

East Porth

ly

West Porth

Innisvouls
Brow

Seal Rock

Innisvouls Neck

Little
Arthur

Outer Carn

Great Innisvouls

Ladies' Ledge Neck

Menawethan Neck

Ladies'
Ledge

Menawethan

Entrance Graves
Arthur Porth

Ragged Island

Arthur Brow

The Hole
The Peak

Renny

China
Point

r Arthur Head

Frenchman's Rock

Eastern Isles

0   0.5   1km

0   1/4   1/2 mile

Plants of Scilly

Stonecrop

Sea Campion

Thrift

Western Gorse

Common Centaury

Lousewort

Island plants

Like all islands the flora of Scilly is dominated by specialist maritime plants. The granite soils are nutrient poor but it is loss of moisture that is the major problem for any plant in this exposed habitat. A whole ecosystem of specialised plants and animals have adapted to turn this problem to their advantage. Most are adapted to increase their ability to retain precious water and in this respect they mimic the adaptations of desert plants - small, waxy, fleshy leaves to reduce transpiration and store water; low growing, dwarfed or prostrate habits where the wind is slower and where ground cover reduces the drying out of the soil and a short growing season triggered by favourable conditions. In fact many are often so completely adapted they are unable to grow or compete in more fertile, sheltered areas. These specialists are a delight to any plant lover.

Plants of the cliff & down

Inhospitable headlands and exposed granite carns crown all the islands. Perhaps the most noticeable feature of the granite carns is the luxuriant growth of the green bearded lichen Ramalina. It can completely cloak the massive granite boulders and obviously luxuriates in the clean, moist atmosphere of Scilly. On the same headlands Thrift or Sea Pink is often found growing out of the smallest crack or fissure in the bare rock. On the more sheltered carns Sea Campion, Danish Scurvy Grass and Samphire compete with the thrift and Sea Mayweed is often found in sheltered corners in the Summer. On the cliffs English Stonecrop grows on the slightest area of weathered granite and in the short turf Common Centaury and Sea Carrot are often found. As shelter increases the turf gives way to bracken. In Spring a woodland type ecosystem flourishes here - Bluebells, Violets and Brambles take advantage of the light before the Bracken shades them out in the Summer. The Brambles are the bane of anyone pushing through the bracken to find archaeological sites which are all but lost by August. On the windswept downs a thin soil allows gnarled, stunted prostrate Heathers to grow often accompanied by Lousewort a hemi-parasite growing off the roots of the Heather. Western Gorse dominates wide areas of the Downs. Its yellow pea flowers open all year round. They have a wonderful almost overpowering coconut scent on still Spring days.